THE LIBRARY O

ISBN: 978-1-5400-4202-6

Visit Hal Leonard Online at
www.halleonard.com

Contact us:
Hal Leonard
7777 West Bluemound Road
Milwaukee, WI 53213
Email: info@halleonard.com

In Europe, contact:
Hal Leonard Europe Limited
42 Wigmore Street
Marylebone, London, W1U 2RY
Email: info@halleonardeurope.com

In Australia, contact:
Hal Leonard Australia Pty. Ltd.
4 Lentara Court
Cheltenham, Victoria, 3192 Australia
Email: info@halleonard.com.au

THE LIBRARY OF

DISNEY SONGS

CONTENTS

THE ARISTOCATS
from THE ARISTOCATS

Words and Music by RICHARD M. SHERMAN
and ROBERT B. SHERMAN

8

ALICE IN WONDERLAND

from ALICE IN WONDERLAND

Words by BOB HILLIARD
Music by SAMMY FAIN

THE BARE NECESSITIES

from THE JUNGLE BOOK

Words and Music by TERRY GILKYSON

THE BALLAD OF DAVY CROCKETT
from DAVY CROCKETT

Words by TOM BLACKBURN
Music by GEORGE BRUNS

1. Born on a moun-tain top in Ten - nes - see, green - est state in the
2. eight - een - thir - teen the Creeks up - rose, add - in' red - skin ar - rows to the
3. Off through the woods _ he's a march - in' a - long, mak - in' up yarns an' a-
4.–10. *(See additional lyrics)*

Land of the Free. Raised in the woods so's he knew ev - 'ry tree,
coun - try's _ woes. Now, In - jun fight - in' is some - thin' he knows, so he
sing - in' a song, itch - in' fer fight - in' and right - in' a wrong, he's

18

Additional Lyrics

4. Andy Jackson is our gen'ral's name,
   His reg'lar soldiers we'll put to shame,
   Them redskin varmints us Volunteers'll tame,
   'Cause we got the guns with the sure-fire aim.
   Davy – Davy Crockett,
   The champion of us all!

5. Headed back to war from the ol' home place,
   But Red Stick was leadin' a merry chase,
   Fightin' an' burnin' at a devil's pace
   South to the swamps on the Florida Trace.
   Davy – Davy Crockett,
   Trackin' the redskins down!

6. Fought single-handed through the Injun War
   Till the Creeks was whipped an' peace was in store,
   An' while he was handlin' this risky chore,
   Made hisself a legend forevermore.
   Davy – Davy Crockett,
   King of the wild frontier!

7. He give his word an' he give his hand
   That his Injun friends could keep their land,
   An' the rest of his life he took the stand
   That justice was due every redskin band.
   Davy – Davy Crockett,
   Holdin' his promise dear!

8. Home fer the winter with his family,
   Happy as squirrels in the ol' gum tree,
   Bein' the father he wanted to be,
   Close to his boys as the pod an' the pea.
   Davy – Davy Crockett,
   Holdin' his young 'uns dear!

9. But the ice went out an' the warm winds came
   An' the meltin' snow showed tracks of game,
   An' the flowers of Spring filled the woods with flame,
   An' all of a sudden life got too tame.
   Davy – Davy Crockett,
   Headin' on West again!

10. Off through the woods we're ridin' along,
    Makin' up yarns an' singin' a song.
    He's ringy as a b'ar and twice as strong,
    An' knows he's right 'cause he ain't often wrong.
    Davy – Davy Crockett,
    The man who don't know fear!

11. Lookin' fer a place where the air smells clean,
    Where the tree is tall an' the grass is green,
    Where the fish is fat in an untouched stream,
    An' the teemin' woods is a hunter's dream.
    Davy – Davy Crockett,
    Lookin' fer Paradise!

12. Now he'd lost his love an' his grief was gall.
    In his heart he wanted to leave it all,
    An' lose himself in the forests tall,
    But he answered instead his country's call.
    Davy – Davy Crockett,
    Beginnin' his campaign!

13. Needin' his help they didn't vote blind,
    They put in Davy 'cause he was their kind,
    Sent up to Nashville the best they could find,
    A fightin' spirit an' a thinkin' mind.
    Davy – Davy Crockett,
    Choice of the whole frontier!

14. The votes were counted an' he won hands down,
    So they sent him off to Washin'ton town
    With his best dress suit still his buckskins brown,
    A livin' legend of growin' renown.
    Davy – Davy Crockett,
    The Canebrake Congressman!

15. He went off to Congress an' served a spell,
    Fixin' up the Gover'ment an' laws as well,
    Took over Washin'ton so we heered tell
    An' patched up the crack in the Liberty Bell.
    Davy – Davy Crockett,
    Seein' his duty clear!

16. Him an' his jokes travelled all through the land,
    An' his speeches made him friends to beat the band,
    His politickin' was their favorite brand
    An' everyone wanted to shake his hand.
    Davy – Davy Crockett,
    Helpin' his legend grow!

17. He knew when he spoke he sounded the knell
    Of his hopes for White House an' fame as well,
    But he spoke out strong so hist'ry books tell
    An' patched up the crack in the Liberty Bell.
    Davy – Davy Crockett,
    Seein' his duty clear!

BEAUTY AND THE BEAST

from BEAUTY AND THE BEAST

Music by ALAN MENKEN
Lyrics by HOWARD ASHMAN

BIBBIDI-BOBBIDI-BOO
(THE MAGIC SONG)
from CINDERELLA

Words by JERRY LIVINGSTON
Music by MACK DAVID and AL HOFFMAN

CAN YOU FEEL THE LOVE TONIGHT
from THE LION KING

Music by ELTON JOHN
Lyrics by TIM RICE

Pop Ballad

There's a calm sur - ren - der
There's a time for ev - 'ry - one,

to the rush of day,
if they on - ly learn

when the heat of the roll - ing world
that the twist - ing ka - lei - do - scope

can be turned a - way.
moves us all in turn.

An en - chant - ed mo - ment,
There's a rhyme and rea - son

CANDLE ON THE WATER

from PETE'S DRAGON

Words and Music by AL KASHA
and JOEL HIRSCHHORN

Smoothly

I'll be your can-dle on the wa-ter, my love for you will al-ways 'til ev-'ry wave is warm and

burn. I know you're lost and drift-ing, but the clouds are lift-ing.
bright. My soul is there be-side you, let this can-dle guide you;

Don't give up; you have some-where to turn.
soon you'll see a gold-en stream of light.

CHIM CHIM CHER-EE

from MARY POPPINS

Words and Music by RICHARD M. SHERMAN
and ROBERT B. SHERMAN

CIRCLE OF LIFE

from THE LION KING

Music by ELTON JOHN
Lyrics by TIM RICE

It's the cir - cle __ of life,

and it moves us all _____ through de - spair and __

COLORS OF THE WIND

from POCAHONTAS

Music by ALAN MENKEN
Lyrics by STEPHEN SCHWARTZ

To Coda ⊕

CRUELLA DE VIL
from 101 DALMATIANS

Words and Music by MEL LEVEN

DO YOU WANT TO BUILD A SNOWMAN?

from FROZEN

Music and Lyrics by KRISTEN ANDERSON-LOPEZ
and ROBERT LOPEZ

A DREAM IS A WISH YOUR HEART MAKES

from CINDERELLA

Music by MACK DAVID and AL HOFFMAN
Lyrics by JERRY LIVINGSTON

EV'RYBODY WANTS TO BE A CAT

from THE ARISTOCATS

Words by FLOYD HUDDLESTON
Music by AL RINKER

EVERMORE

from BEAUTY AND THE BEAST

Music by ALAN MENKEN
Lyrics by TIM RICE

GO THE DISTANCE

from HERCULES

Music by ALAN MENKEN
Lyrics by DAVID ZIPPEL

GOD HELP THE OUTCASTS

from THE HUNCHBACK OF NOTRE DAME

Music by ALAN MENKEN
Lyrics by STEPHEN SCHWARTZ

Eb(add9)
Cm7
Bb/F
F
hun - gry from birth. Show them the mer - cy they
I can get by. But I know so man - y less
Bbsus
Bb
F/A
Gm
F/G
don't find on Earth. The lost and for - got - ten, they
luck - y than I. God help the out - casts, the
Cm7
Ebm6
Bb/F
look to You still. God help the out - casts or
poor and down - trod. I thought we all were the
F7b9
1
Bb
Bbmaj7
Eb/Bb
Bb
no - bod - y will.
chil - dren of

83

HE'S A TRAMP

from LADY AND THE TRAMP

Words and Music by PEGGY LEE
and SONNY BURKE

HOW DOES A MOMENT LAST FOREVER

from BEAUTY AND THE BEAST

Music by ALAN MENKEN
Lyrics by TIM RICE

How ____ does a mo-ment last for - ev - er? _____ How can a sto-ry ____ nev - er

HOW FAR I'LL GO

from MOANA

Music and Lyrics by LIN-MANUEL MIRANDA

HAPPY WORKING SONG

from ENCHANTED

Music by ALAN MENKEN
Lyrics by STEPHEN SCHWARTZ

I JUST CAN'T WAIT TO BE KING

from THE LION KING

Music by ELTON JOHN
Lyrics by TIM RICE

I SEE THE LIGHT

from TANGLED

Music by ALAN MENKEN
Lyrics by GLENN SLATER

Moderately

I WAN'NA BE LIKE YOU
(THE MONKEY SONG)
from THE JUNGLE BOOK

Words and Music by RICHARD M. SHERMAN
and ROBERT B. SHERMAN

Brightly (with a jungle beat)

Now I'm the king of the swing-ers, the jun-gle V. I.
try to kid me man-cub, and don't get in a
ape your man-ner-is-ms, we'll be a set of

P. I've reached the top and had to stop and
stew. What I de-sire is man's red fire, so
twins. No one will know where man-cub ends and o-

that's what's both-er-in' me. I wan-na be a man, man-cub, and
I can be like you. Give me the se-cret, man-cub, just
rang-u-tan be-gins. And when I eat ba-na-nas, I won't

I'M LATE

from ALICE IN WONDERLAND

Words by BOB HILLIARD
Music by SAMMY FAIN

IT'S A SMALL WORLD

from Disney Parks 'it's a small world' Attraction

Words and Music by RICHARD M. SHERMAN
and ROBERT B. SHERMAN

It's a world of laugh - ter, a world of tears; it's a world of hopes and a world of fears. There's so much that we share that it's time we're a - ware it's a

just one moon and one gold - en sun and a smile means friend - ship to ev - 'ry - one. Though the moun - tains div - ide and the o - ceans are wide, it's a

KISS THE GIRL

from THE LITTLE MERMAID

Music by ALAN MENKEN
Lyrics by HOWARD ASHMAN

IF I NEVER KNEW YOU
(END TITLE)
from POCAHONTAS

Music by ALAN MENKEN
Lyrics by STEPHEN SCHWARTZ

137

I'LL MAKE A MAN OUT OF YOU

from MULAN

Music by MATTHEW WILDER
Lyrics by DAVID ZIPPEL

144

LAVENDER BLUE (DILLY DILLY)

from SO DEAR TO MY HEART

Words by LARRY MOREY
Music by ELIOT DANIEL

LET IT GO

from FROZEN

Music and Lyrics by KRISTEN ANDERSON-LOPEZ
and ROBERT LOPEZ

Gaining confidence

158

MICKEY MOUSE MARCH

from MICKEY MOUSE CLUB

Words and Music by JIMMIE DODD

ONCE UPON A DREAM

from SLEEPING BEAUTY

Words and Music by SAMMY FAIN
and JACK LAWRENCE
Adapted from a Theme by TCHAIKOVSKY

PART OF YOUR WORLD

from THE LITTLE MERMAID

Music by ALAN MENKEN
Lyrics by HOWARD ASHMAN

A PIRATE'S LIFE
from PETER PAN

Words by ED PENNER
Music by OLIVER WALLACE

REMEMBER ME
(ERNESTO DE LA CRUZ)
from COCO

Words and Music by KRISTEN ANDERSON-LOPEZ
and ROBERT LOPEZ

REFLECTION
from MULAN

Music by MATTHEW WILDER
Lyrics by DAVID ZIPPEL

When will my re-flec-tion show who I am in-
Why is my re-flec-tion some-one
Must there be a se-cret me I'm

side?
I am now in a

world where I ___ have to hide my heart __ and what I be-lieve in.

I forced don't to know? hide?

THE SECOND STAR TO THE RIGHT

from PETER PAN

Words by SAMMY CAHN
Music by SAMMY FAIN

Moderately slow

The sec-ond star to the right shines in the night for you,

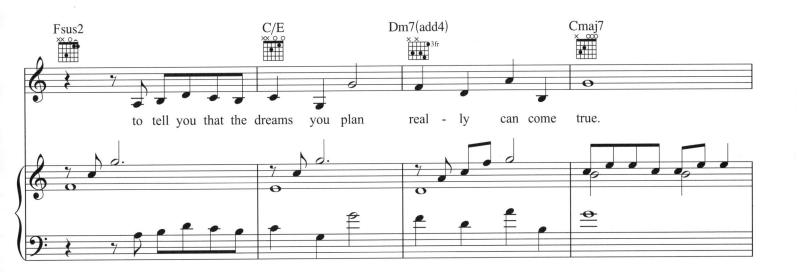

to tell you that the dreams you plan real-ly can come true.

The sec-ond star to the right shines with a light that's

THE SIAMESE CAT SONG

from LADY AND THE TRAMP

Words and Music by PEGGY LEE
and SONNY BURKE

SOMEDAY

from THE HUNCHBACK OF NOTRE DAME

Music by ALAN MENKEN
Lyrics by STEPHEN SCHWARTZ

A SPOONFUL OF SUGAR

from MARY POPPINS

Words and Music by RICHARD M. SHERMAN
and ROBERT B. SHERMAN

193

SUPERCALIFRAGILISTICEXPIALIDOCIOUS
from MARY POPPINS

Words and Music by RICHARD M. SHERMAN
and ROBERT B. SHERMAN

TRASHIN' THE CAMP
(POP VERSION)
from TARZAN®

Words and Music by PHIL COLLINS

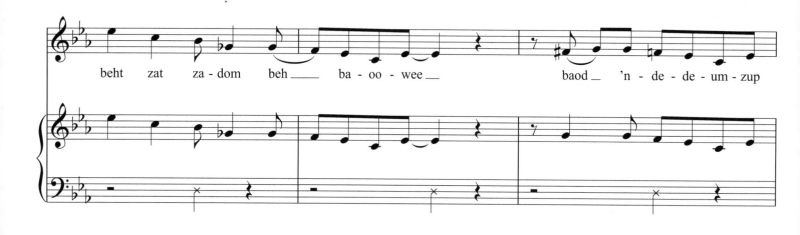

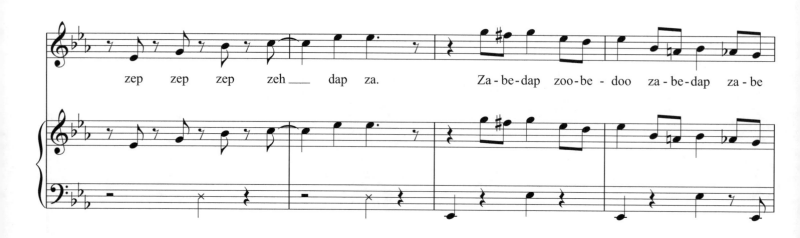

UNDER THE SEA

from THE LITTLE MERMAID

Music by ALAN MENKEN
Lyrics by HOWARD ASHMAN

214

THE UNBIRTHDAY SONG

from ALICE IN WONDERLAND

Words and Music by MACK DAVID,
AL HOFFMAN and JERRY LIVINGSTON

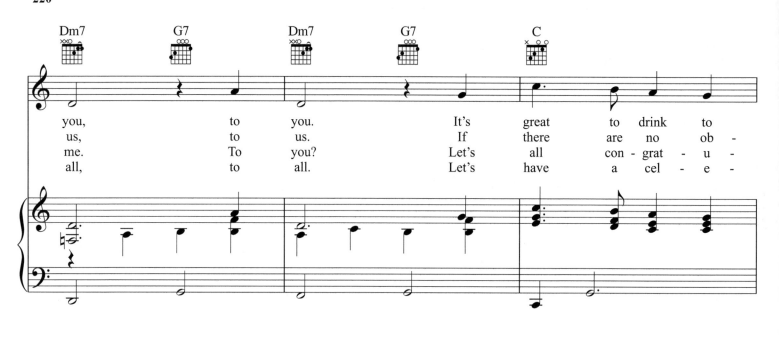

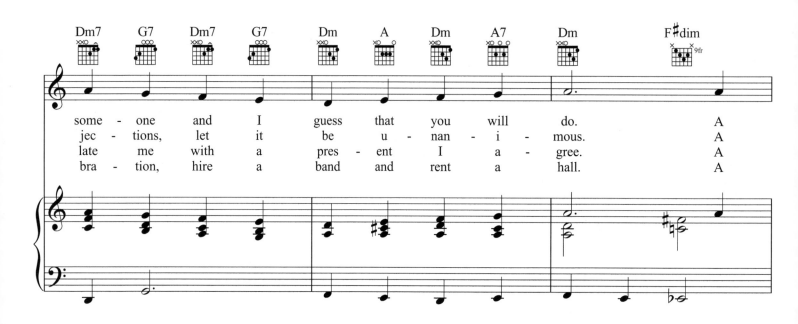

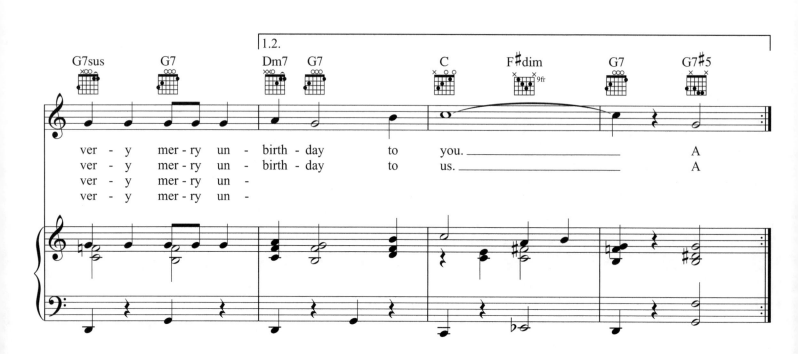

WINNIE THE POOH

from THE MANY ADVENTURES OF WINNIE THE POOH

Words and Music by RICHARD M. SHERMAN
and ROBERT B. SHERMAN

Based on the "Winnie the Pooh" works, by A. A. Milne and E. H. Shepard

A WHALE OF A TALE

from 20,000 LEAGUES UNDER THE SEA

Words and Music by NORMAN GIMBEL
and AL HOFFMAN

WHEN SHE LOVED ME

from TOY STORY 2

Music and Lyrics by RANDY NEWMAN

A WHOLE NEW WORLD
from ALADDIN

Music by ALAN MENKEN
Lyrics by TIM RICE

234

236

WRITTEN IN THE STARS

from AIDA

Music by ELTON JOHN
Lyrics by TIM RICE

239

THE WORLD ES MI FAMILIA

from COCO

Music by GERMAINE FRANCO
Lyrics by ADRIAN MOLINA

YOU'LL BE IN MY HEART
(POP VERSION)
from TARZAN®

Words and Music by PHIL COLLINS

Moderately

Come stop your cry - ing; it will be al - right. Just take my hand,

hold it tight. I will pro-tect you from all a-round you.

I will be here; don't you cry.
For one so small you
Why can't they un-der-stand the

YOU CAN FLY! YOU CAN FLY! YOU CAN FLY!

from PETER PAN

Words by SAMMY CAHN
Music by SAMMY FAIN

256

YOU'VE GOT A FRIEND IN ME

from TOY STORY

Music and Lyrics by RANDY NEWMAN

ZERO TO HERO

from HERCULES

Music by ALAN MENKEN
Lyrics by DAVID ZIPPEL

G C/G G C/G G C/G
les. Whose dar - ing deeds are great the - a - ter? Her - cu -
G B♭ E♭/B♭ 6fr B♭ E♭/B♭ 6fr B♭ D7 Csus2/E
les. Is he bold? No one brav - er. Is he sweet? Our
Fdim7 D7/F♯ G G7/B C D7sus G G7/B
fa - v'rite fla - vor. Her - cu - les. Her - cu -
C D7sus G G7/B C D7sus G G7/B
les. Her - cu - les. Her - cu -

YOU'RE WELCOME

from MOANA

Music and Lyrics by LIN-MANUEL MIRANDA

Additional Lyrics

Rap: Kid, honestly, I could go on and on.
I could explain ev'ry nat'ral phenomenon.
The tide? The grass? The ground?
Oh, that was Maui, just messing around.

I killed an eel, I buried its guts,
Sprouted a tree: now you got coconuts!
What's the lesson? What is the takeaway?
Don't mess with Maui when he's on a breakaway.

And the tapestry here in my skin
Is a map of the vict'ries I win!
Look where I've been! I make ev'rything happen!
Look at that mean mini Maui, just tickety
Tappin'! Heh, heh, heh,
Heh, heh, heh, hey!

DISCOVER OUR RANGE OF FILM SOUNDTRACKS...

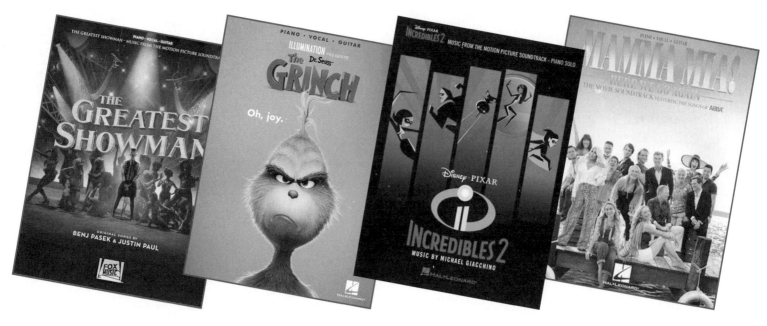

ORDER NO. HL00250373   ORDER NO. HL00288578   ORDER NO. HL00282473   ORDER NO. HL00280953

ORDER NO. HL00286617   ORDER NO. HL00280822   ORDER NO. HL00277134   ORDER NO. HL00285000

ALSO AVAILABLE ONLINE AND FROM ALL GOOD MUSIC SHOPS...

ORDER NO. AM1009712

ORDER NO. HL00233553

ORDER NO. HL00218254

ORDER NO. HL00146042

ORDER NO. HL00257746

ORDER NO. HL00262694

ORDER NO. HL00218878

ORDER NO. HL00255621

ORDER NO. AM1013122

ORDER NO. AM1013661

ORDER NO. HL00243903

ORDER NO. HL00174170

Just visit your local music shop and ask
to see our huge range of music in print.